Dedication

For The People

We can fix our spiritual sicknesses that have come to a head, so they can go into total remission in order to create a rebirth, or new birth, for the world. America can set a precedent by way of the Lord's leadership. We are lined up to follow in faith.

Hello to All

This book and others I have authored have been written for the advancement of all people to create a new America and eliminate the repairs in our lives or government to head off problems from taking place, and save the country millions or even billions of dollars at the same time.

On the flip side, that is the better side, to create a way to prevent hurt, harm, danger and/or death of a multitude of people. This can be done with the Lord's blessings by breaking the bondages of plagues and curses that can be prevented.

The democrats and republicans can use this to help end there warfare of a spiritual kind that most or just about of them has no idea of where it's coming from or going to, because of the nature of the beast that uses people. It does not disclose itself because it does not wont to be detected by its host so it stays on the down low to keep chaos going on in ways it can lead some to create a belief that makes the opposite seem right, whether it may be right or wrong. Just because it's a spell of a pact like in a wolf pack kind of

1

mentality that misplaces their single status of being and living as one.

Could I be right in saying that I somewhat had to put a rush on this book out of desperation to be a part of the new growth of the country to help define an upswing toward brighter days that we all can share in. This will also show the world how much we really care about ourselves and that we are still a blessed nation on the planet earth.

Don't get me wrong my love is developed to bring out the best in all people to be shared with the needy and not the greedy. Unfortunately, there are some people that know that bad time bring about the opportunity for some of the wealthy people to gain more wealth! I personally hope no one has such a sick mind to think like that because we can truly take of our needy and it is time to stop being a part of the greedy. A change has come to dissipate personal problems starting with the Republicans and Democrats!

I WILL BLESS THE LORD

Foreword

This is an introduction to a part of possible solutions to the problems we are facing and how to eliminate them. It is a part of the unraveling of a part of a kaleidoscope of knowledge presented by Bro. Tracy Bush it's a presentation of work to help others become wiser.

Please America: Take the Blinders Off!

It is time to stop walking through, or living in, the valley of ignorance that has been placed in the USA.

Take Notice

While our country is busy worrying about terrorists from outside or within our boundaries, we should be concerned about towerists that are in our country, some of which are in powerful positions.

From T.B.

American people,
you make me feel like I am alive again!

Let us Meet at A Point of Mutual Understanding!

M-N

In the USA, I like to stop thinking there is something going on that makes my skin tie up in a knot; that can be stopped.

A New Flight to A New Height

Is this a part of a new harvest of wisdom? Leviticus 23 –22 says, "When you reap the harvest of your land, you shall not wholly reap the corners of your field when you reap, nor shall you gather any gleaning from your harvest. You shall leave them for the poor and for the stranger: I am the Lord your God."

Off The Pathway

To cure a sickness caused by a toweritis will require a towerectomy to help stop the business as usual, of someone who is trying to become something like a politician or president that never been in that avenue of growth, because running a country is not like a business.

This book is a non-fictional editorial. No permission has been given by any of the people who have been named. This is an unauthorized document. Please stop and listen.

Welcome to a Peace Process

Now if the book was also written by the Parekletòs, it has to have a large part of it that has life within it. Therefore, let's say it's life force is a sounding instrument of miracles and it plays a tune that is leading the dirty spirit away out of mankind to a place where it can no longer hurt anyone. We sing along saying "bye-bye darkness, I am glad to know you are gone. I thank you Holy Spirit that you came along to save a part of me I didn't know was gone. Bye-bye darkness, I am truly glad you are gone.

Did the Lord give this wisdom to mankind to help put the country back on track by showing them what it is to be in a spiritual war with a person who has towerism? Also showing the country how to defeat the harry-carry mayhem that has been created by them that has caused a calamity that can bust a party apart. Did the Lord supply the wisdom to stop this kind of filibuster from happening to the Congress of the USA Republican party? Yes, he did will they accept it? The jury is still out.

Does or can the wisdom that the Lord gave to one man to share help put the country back on track after all this time it has been off track? Time will tell.

The writing I am commissioned to do isn't to single out to defeat anyone but it is to unite us all in our democracy to help equip us on a level to help us all live better with each other.

The process of not letting our democracy become defeated by a spiritual warfare is the mission I have been commissioned to show the people how to win. The grunt work has been done, all it takes is applying the wisdom; with understanding one word that can't be found in the dictionary, "towerism."

Now can we all go into a successful prelude?

How did the problem with the government and the people get started? I will not go into a lot of details, but it has been around since almost the beginning of time.

To clear up even more about what towerism is and can be: a person with towerism is somewhat like a baby terrorist that keeps itself somewhat in an innocent state of presence. It does its best to not let their unclean hand be seen or detected by the people who they are around, unless they are their partner in crime. In most cases they find a way to keep it legal even though it is somewhat or it is shady dealing that can and may rob some people blind. That calls for 411 and not 911, if you need more proof that the unhealthy people don't need to be in control of our lives as leaders. People with towerism never should have the right to control a segment of our population but they did and now the time has come to stop letting them. It is up to the people to stop this.

The cousin of towerism is named dictatorship a complete rundown about the family of dysfunctional development that the power of darkness resides in can be found in the book *The Recovery of the U.S. Government*.

What Does All This Mean?

It is a way to break the greed-lock before it is another gridlock as it was in 1952 within the Republican party. The word "towerism" was brought forth to identify a place where people sit up high in, that can and may create an unhealthy way of life for others. There may be many ways to say how wrong they can be for the people. It makes no sense, even with malicious words they say to others. The people need to stop wasting time and money of the people who pay their salary in our country.

Stopping towerism: how do we do this? by learning the process of elimination of the powerful strangers that is with in some people that need to be stopped or if we become or if we are aware we are one with the problems than change our ways that are wrong.

It is time to stop overreaching to find something that is already at hand. Know that when you fight against evil with your good and you are not completely equipped, you may act out as they do before they change. It can become an unhealthy path so stay off of it in a fight you may be out of wind before you win.

Once you have finished this manual Tweet out the information, if you have any faith in this message.

A Sweet Smell

It is time to believe in something that may not be totally explained at the beginning of the learning that we can show our trust in so truth will reveal itself. The process in the books that are linked to one another are like the pedals on a flower that make up the whole flower. They grow together as one even though they seem separate somewhat. So are the books I write that become as one in times, as time goes on. It is time for the people to be careful because we could knock our own country on its ass by us acting like asses and letting the country act like an ass and letting the country be run by one is crazy!

What Do People With Towerism Do As A Team?

When they gather towers together, they block, stop and sometimes act like haters so others won't get their way. They stop things or push others' agenda aside to get what they want. When there is a pack of them they love to overshadow to defeat other parties and even the president. If you look at some of them too long you may see the flea flicking fur bearing varmint they turn into at times.

To end the problem of towerism in this country, we need a double edged sword to fix the unseen concerns of the cancer with spiritual surgery. It took two parties to create this issue and both have to accept the blame, both the people and the government. We can fix this by doing our homework.

In order to know, they can learn when they are near to hear and see it in someone in a certain period of time. To also know you have the power to overcome any advances from the person with towerism to cut it out of your life in whatever way is needed, in order for anyone to start to rejuvenate and revitalize the country. Stop the madness and sadness in order to bring about some gladness, happiness to and for our nation.

Did the people in America need a reason to wake up and tip the scales? We must have. Now that the politicians see that the Americans are fed up with their bullshit, they are willing to put a clump in the office to work things out and that is a big mistake. Now because of this they may come down out of their own towers and do the right thing. Some of them have been so stuck up on a perch that it has now created a level of a downfall that may and could hurt the party in ways that may or may not ever get repaired again. If that doesn't make them wise, the failure to realize their own kind from another dimension can sneak up in their lair where they feel is impenetrable and harm them. It has happened and they are in shock.

Therefore, wake up everybody and look at the mess we may be blessed to get out of, if we stop the towerism. Also to the people and voters, if you think this country is messed up now, just wait to see. I take that back, you don't want to see what could happen if a clump gets into office by electing towerists.

We can redevelop our faith in the political system of America. You don't have to get stuck with the clump as your ass. Get out of the hole. Even though you are in some kind of quicksand, BTHPM will help through a way to redevelop our faith. If we don't the USA will catch hell and go through it.

At BTHPM, we do what we do to help the people. We want people to look at themselves and see if what we show them in the information can improve their lives. It is for everyone and we agree to disagree with people through and about some ideas and hold no malice against them because we can wish everyone well. It doesn't hurt anything to have a good expression to project at anyone.

Now knowing that America has come to its turning point, whose point of view will you let influence you, the good, the bad or the ugly. I hope none of the above. I hope you find a heartfelt presence of righteousness to rely on and share with an unconditional love for all the people on earth, even the ones who are enemies to themselves who want to share it with you.

As a country, it seems like we have bigger fish to fry but it seems like we are frying ourselves. Therefore, let's get out of the frying pan before we start serving burned fish up to each other.

Now is it up to the Democratic Party to save the country from the clump and also the republican party from the pain of not being able to get their heads out of the clump butts because they never saw the clump coming. That shows them when you are up so high in a tower how blind you get. Be thankful you can get another chance at winning again so don't be sad or mad at each other.

Author's Note

Voters – at one time my mind ran like a big jumbotron at the movies. Now it runs like a big teleconference to put out the information that is needed and/or if we were a republican and did not want a tower in the White House, are we strong enough to use a democrat as president to become our friend?

Republicans

Now can you be thankful and humble that someone is there to save your asses?

Now that the Republican Party has demanded the labeling on one of theirs they had ignored and counted out the one thing they can't stop now is its quacking like a duck. They had no idea it would put itself in a position where they seem mindless on how to shut it up.

But never fear help is here. He is of the same kind of cloth as some of you are blind to see he is a tower and it is meant to fall by way of the blindness that is shared with all who follow. What is that one fact that they always forget? You are not Heaven's best, you just got blessed. The Lord is in control and not anyone else and if he said you won't win, you won't. I believe in what He says but it takes the people believe in themselves to make it true ask not what the Lord can do for you but what you can do for the Lord. Make this come true.

In other words, it is time to stop what the Lord saves us from all the time from. We can save ourselves. If we don't we can't blame the Lord because He has given us dominion over the earth and it is inhabitants to rule as he would if he had to do everything himself. Therefore it is our turn to turn up our faith into works.

One question: if the Lord gives us all an ability to do something what did he give you to do with what you have? If you don't know, ask, he will tell you then use it.

If one party saw what happened to the other party because of their arrogance, they can learn from it. Now knowing when one person makes a mistake and no one learns from then everybody is wrong for it like it or not!

We can or we must get over ourselves and forgive ourselves and our country for what we may have done to ourselves. We can be and have been blind somewhat but we are still united in our efforts to create a better life for all people, even though there are still a few bitter seeds. Hear now if the people are truly tired and fed up with the way this county has been going and run by big business and the government. This may be one of its greatest ways to have a chance for the people to make change under the blessing of the Lord.

Today

We can change the articles of bias out of the constitution that are in between the lines we don't see. Now is the time to claim and share the riches of the world without the wealth of money to come between it that towerism has taken from some of the people in our country. Now is the time for all people to be aware of the blind who can lead the blind. It may be like an anti-Christ who comes just testing the water.

Could this be some kind of test run that Satan is making to see where our heads are at or is it the Lord wanting to see where our hearts are? Is it a level of both that wants to see how much the people love America or how much they love towerists?

How to win this war on a spiritual level: with the Lord leading the way. He has given us all that we need. Now will we use it? I say yes! But if the unwise doesn't know, how can we protect them except with our love.

The Truth of it All to My Brother's Keeper

If we have a threat made against us by a foreign country, we respond with defense. Therefore, if it is a citizen who does it, do we find a better way to respond or do we just let them do something and get away with it? Hell no! We handle it in the right way if we keep the law on our side and if mankind's laws won't establish one of the laws, a law needs to be put in place for towerism.

Now Let it be Known

The Lord heard the battle cries and he sent his warriors, not with traditional weapons, but by the pen which is mightier or greater than the sword to lead the charge and defeat the enemy and to keep the peace in the world in the name of the Lord. There is a battle cry out for exterior and interior to join the rally to defeat the foul and take the spoils back from the crooks that tried to take over the country. We need not say much more about what can't be done.

As far as the recovery again it starts at the U.S. government, it also starts with people and the country's economy. This is a part of the spiritual skills development process that can help make this come to a truth. Now is the time to claim and share the richness of the world without the wealth of money to come between it.

Plop, Plop, Fizz, Fizz

It is a relief to know that the Lord has equipped his soldiers and girded them up to defeat the enemy, as it was when the last president had his second time around whether some liked it or not!

The people of a certain state of mind call their campaign funds a war chest. This is a war chest that is not fueled by money but by the love the people have for this country. You can't or no one can beat that, especially if it has been sanctioned by the Lord.

Now is the right time to create the death of "isms," such as political "isms" that attract towerists to it and are tied into towerism that also attracts terrorists.

A Word or More

I advise all people to keep the Lord is in front of you in all battles. Satan slips up into the spiritual one that people get caught off guard with and lose.

From a strut to a stumble we dump the Clump! Have a place for people to help tweet him out.

Warning

Beware and stop it before it gets voted in a position that creates the wanting of terrorists to come to America and not in the name of Jesus. We should never play at a time when we can stop the straw that may break the camel's back. The back is America and the straw is a clump that may bring us lack that sets us back in life also add back luck to it all. It is, or may be like inventing a prelude to an anti-Christ like element into the greatest position in the free world.

Dump the Clump
See and Know

Voting power of the people of our country has taken on a new face that it has never known before. Therefore, it may be somewhat a spiritual war that we can win with the Lord.

Personally, we can determine the elected president, because we don't have to be careless as voters. Prayer for the right leader in the White House is what we will get if we put in the work to make this happen. The savings of money that is wasted can create job training and employment.

President Obama has recently introduced legislation to Congress for $11 billion to help combat terrorism. This may not be funded until later 2016 or after. Once it can be used the cost of its uses can be cut to less than half.

Bump anyone who practices towerism
out of the race to be a politician

It is hard to change someone with toweritis that is in the habit of building towers in their name. Now the bad part of when a tower falls as was shown in those who used the ponzy schemes is how many are hurt because of this.

A Pound of Prevention

They say nothing ever happens without a crisis and this is one thing that we can get under control. To prevent one we have to have insight and do something about it with action. Do you want to know the preventive measures being created through this message?

At This Time My Mind Is Running Like a
Jumbotron So All Can Know

How much money can also be saved by using the book *The Disconnection of Extremism*, to help eliminate the radicalization of people? How much can be used on other things the USA needs to have done also that can be saved to aid to the understanding of this, book *The Recovery of the U.S. Government*, to clean up within the White House first that help others not want to dirty up or harm America?

This

If we were a republican and didn't want a tower in the White House maybe we should choose a democratic president. Therefore, if we pray for the right leader in the White House that is what we will get. Promoting these causes can help save an important part of the White House. This is to help appoint the best candidate possible not the lesser of two evils.

A Miracle That is Real

I can use this scenario if someone is stuck on someone else's "ism" it can be called, let's say clumpism, which causes clumpitis requiring them to have a clumpectomy to cure them and save them from themselves.

Read this with love: 1 Timothy 1:1-11

2 Timothy 4:6-8
6. For I am already being poured out as a drink offering, and the time of my departure is at hand.
7. I have fought the good fight, I have finished the race, I have kept the faith.
8. Finally, there is laid up for me the crown of righteousness, which the Lord, the righteous Judge, will give to me on that Day, and not to me only but also to all who have loved His appearing.

New Days

Put together a new level of work on a campaign to defeat any kind of Donald Duck Clump. See a worthwhile fight get in it.

People, you have been told: you would be better off with "Erkelism" than towerism!

This wisdom releases the presence of a kind of ghetto logic that people may be able to use.

Author's Note
I Admit

One of the problems I have with my writing is it is more so for the spiritual consciousness and not just for the entertainment of mankind.

A man could be three things: what others thinks he is; what he thinks he is; or what he really is.

We are still on the march, in ways, for equality we need to fix in all humanity. We are just touching the surface about that. We have been living in the dark.

It is my thought and my opinion that if there is not a chance to put the desired person of my independent choice in the White House and I see where they will not succeed in getting elected, I would rather switch than fight a losing battle to another party to invite the best candidate into the job on the other side, even if it is a change of my party choice of someone else in the opposite party.

We can help each other grow up within a new stage in the political arena before the new commander in chief gets in office. Therefore, the people will know who to look for and give their rightful vote to see humanity prosper and save the souls of people, because sometimes truth when spoken gets people killed.

All isn't lost and we can learn how to change the mindset of the wrong person if they enter the office of the presidency. This is the Lord's will.

As some would say when there is no fail-proof program that guarantees there will not be mistakes made in the judgment of building a referendum for political policies in government. To have this new kind of additional measure of God's blessing with the belief of him surpasses all of mankind's understanding is all we can hope for at times in life, whether we see it or not on paper when it is planted in our hearts. This can be all that we can hope for at times, no buts about it.

L.B.J. was a president and lots of people were surprised when he got into office because they knew him as somewhat of a non-caring person toward certain minorities. But when he got elected he helped to create justice for all people.

Therefore, a job can change people but he was also experienced in what it took to become a politician. Some things are not so possible if you don't know how in the first place. If you have the curse of towerism as a possible way of life, a job can change that for you.

The changing of the commander in chief comes every so often in our lifetimes. Now to prepare for it is up to us. How can we become wiser if it is an unwise president with towerism put in the White House? First, know what their problems are. If they are not afflicted with towerism, we can see their heart as a person. If they have a dark side of blinding others to a truth, that needs to be fixed. We still can work with facts to improve life for all.

They need help. Time will tell how we will know what to do and the people they work with will know and tell the truth about what is in their hearts. If we stand together and be seen as a light we can show the way out of a dark side to the forerunners that are to lead the country into a better life for all mankind.

To help government workers get away from the curse of blindness, teach them to not respect it. It is a force that can and will over power people on all levels on all sides of the government with the ending of towerism.

The Birth of Spiritual Skills is Being Renewed

Freedom to claim victory over problems that some people can't (or won't) see and selfishness helps keep them from, is here. The truth of what may be the right thing to do is available. Does this need a part of the written law of our country's constitution? I think so.

Therapy Information

The plague of towerism that politicians created is not addressed within the soul of mankind that should be because they or some need help to stop it in them, and this can help, *The Recovery of the U.S. Government, (The Power of Knowing "No")*, to help end towerism in government because the running of the country shouldn't be treated like a business, or a place that disrupts peoples' lives. It should be treated like a living, breathing human being because that is what it is made of. If the economy takes a fall because of the new regime that sets a wrong person in place in the White House, and the less fortunate are hit with the penalty of towerism, who will suffer the most? The poor people, as always.

Therefore, what can we do to help assure this won't happen? Take steps to give them a chance. Note: this is another kind of peace offering to and for the protection from towerism because it is a desire and plague combining the power of greed with selfishness.

The problem with towerism is when some people get infected with it, it is like getting on an elevator and they go straight up to the top in their mindset and don't have an idea how to stop it and get off. The book is like a visit to the doctor's office to help them get down out of it and/or a hospital visit to know of a sickness to receive an anecdote.

Like skills, gets skills!

This is a part of why people don't tell themselves the truth about everything. One reason they don't know that the Lord has me building a lighthouse to get people out of the tower with spiritual skills. It gives the vision of taking a sled down a ski slope and not falling off and getting hurt.

Who is the most likely kind of person to get towerism? It is the person in a business who gets affected the most. At one time, it was the church who had a problem with this some of the clergy didn't accept it. But the worse people on earth with it are the dictators and the so-called leaders in foreign countries, especially third world countries.

There are other plan programs to advance the people out of the unpromised lands or stages of life and some can work but which one is right for you? It is somewhat of a trial level of work. Do I believe in me? With this wisdom to be used in my life and sometimes people want to put a little in only and expect a lot out of it. Therefore be for real enough to know what you will get out of what you put in and don't make an excuse for it, then try to put the blame on anything but yourself.

Which is The Most Precious?

If someone has a light bulb in hand what is the first thing they think about? If they are an able bodied person, it is to know what its purpose is. Also it is to handle it with care in order to not break it because if it is broken it no longer has a purpose. If that happens it becomes useless and the price that was paid for it is a loss before is usefulness has come to pass. It will not have a past and the light it can supply will not shine. Even though every part of it and its purpose has a time to no longer give light once it is in place. We want it to live out its longevity in order to make it a valuable part of our life to help us see in the dark.

Therefore, we take care not to crack the light bulb. If it is a child who has the task of placing it where it needs to be and they are not equipped to do the job and break it. Unfortunately, it becomes useless and all they feel is that they have cracked their bulb.

If we as a people are in need of that light we need to seek it before it becomes lost forever. It didn't give us what we need. So let's look at mankind and its purpose if we need to help light the way for each other and we crack our bulb when it's our time to light the way for ourselves and others, it is a loss of light that we are supposed to shine for ourselves and others.

How do we feel being left in the dark? Not good: therefore, to become an adult in life, we should not crack our bulb. What is our bulb? It is the light that comes out of our mind sight that comes from the heart of mankind to show the way out of darkness into light.

What ways do we do this? It is by not creating harm, heartaches and/or pain that we give out to others, whether it comes from a misunderstanding that has a level of conflict within it that blinds us from the truth, along with the facts that we can't see or know how to believe in the truth that is set forth in front of us. We are still children in a way we don't want to admit that so we crack our bulb, the bulb that has a child handling it, and not an adult.

Before we become an adult in life, we must know the child in us that is a child of Christ Jesus. It teaches us to be able to know how to handle our light bulb that we have been blessed with.

Therefore, which is the most important to you, the manmade one or the one you have been blessed with? How do you handle them both? Do you trust you to do this or do you trust the Lord to work with you in order to not break either one? Do you use your judgment alone to not screw the bulb in the wrong way and to not screw yourself or others? Are you alone with the light leading your way or are you in the dark by yourself in your thinking? Did you make the bulb by yourself? Did you make your life by yourself?

If you did, you are in darkness or do you recognize you are not alone? Even so, it took others to help me write this message with ink and paper and the light of two sons, son to help keep me out of darkness that I depend on.

God bless you whoever may read this. Additionally, as a part of our saving grace we be better off if before we crack our God given light bulb, about anything, we break the manmade one as therapeutic or as a stress reliever.

Author's Note

What I write could be a way for the people to not just go into a way to understand darkness but to come out of darkness? I think so, to turn on the bulb after putting it in the right way. What can be one of our biggest game plans? It is to divide our personal problems one at a time, with ourselves, to conquer it instead of thinking our life is one big problem. We do this by saying "I am the righteousness of the Lord because this is who we are," in His reality and not the worldliness that created a mess at times in our lives.

We never need to think of ourselves as a legend in our own minds. It makes us think too highly of ourselves. People that may have this may be affected by towerism. A more detailed explanation of this is in the government book *The Recovery of The U.S. Government (The Power of Knowing "No"*.

The Dangers in America We Can Fix

You need to understand also if you think a tower that only wont power is a joke, give it some though it can attract people whether there right or wrong because of their ability to make money blinds people that wont to be like them or close to them.

Who needs to become the wiser in helping to stop the manmade plagues and/or curses we put upon ourselves as humans? Do we need to keep looking the other way when we know how to stop a problem before it starts? The good that comes out of evil isn't worth the trial and error it possesses.

The problem that some of the people in all branches have had with towerism causes the attacks on Americans that toppled down the twin towers. If we have a tower present in leading us, it will attract more people like that that may want try to want to do us harm in the USA. This is my feeling and I hope I am wrong but time will tell. Therefore, let's not have to clean house at the same time we are making a mess of it.

So Be It

If we are the greatest country in the world, then why do we have one of the greatest levels of foolishness? I think it is because of the educated foolishness of people in their own tower who are truly out of touch with the common man then they also left their duties as a brother's keeper, to a level of pinning it on the clergy to do and they can't do it by themselves because it is an all people duty.

The Plague

Talking about the water problem or as it has in Brazil that there government should have been on top of before it got out of hand. That is in Michigan was caused by the people with towerism. Stop the people with towerism and stop the manmade plagues.

What Do You Think?

To help the world: if we the small people don't try to untie the knot that can hold us back in life then nobody else can help us with stopping towerism unless we help ourselves.

It may not have been nice to have been the one who brought a new dimension of reality into the vision of the mindset of people. That may leave a bitter taste into someone's growth pattern, but without it some of the people might perish that can be saved. Therefore, I say hallelujah to this.

I have been someone who has felt somewhat locked into contributing to the democratic party all of my life. That is why I say at any time in your reading this you may be required of yourself to take a brief intermission to clear your vision; because if need be, I can change over.

We present the facts of what make the people lose faith in the leaders on a laymen terminology to recreate the order that came from the Lord and not mankind at this time. To think so or to think too strongly, gives me reason to keep moving on.

Just Imagine

If one man can come up with help to save our government with a reality check to get things in a more orderly format, it can only be done by the will of

God. Therefore, don't hate the messenger because it needed to be done.

To Help the Country

We can't and shouldn't put ourselves in a position as if we are sitting ducks in the water. We must become busy in the spirit of changing course. If we can see what could be the trouble ahead of us and not do a thing about it, we are blind and foolish and we are not using common sense. Can we agree to disagree on this?

Now if one party can't win give yourself an "A" for another candidate, because we can keep this democracy's growth going stronger.

A Better Look

Now how many blows for justice can we make to take out injustices in our country? The possibilities are endless that can last forever. It is time for the people in the USA to stop being frustrated by the government and now this may be one way out. Within these pages you have to determine how to categorize what needs to go where.

As For The Police and People: Hear This

This may be one of the best help-mates for the police. The cities are doing something for the police but not for the attitude of the people. Millions of dollars are spent, but not for the people to help their wounds, their inner pain and hurt. As always, what are you doing to help the people because they need a better understanding of how to fix the way they feel?

To Take a Break and Not Get Lost Into One's Self, We Think About Others

How many cop haters still don't give a damn and want to hurt the police? What are we doing to help them with their problem or dilemma? Nothing much but at BTHPM there is the book, _A Peace Offering for the Police and the People_, that can help. If there is time to help it won't hurt the police to know the way it can help.

Now is This a Good Reason to be Grateful?

Most "Billy bad ass" cops have been scared straight due to cameras or them not wanting to get in trouble. We are spending tax dollars to protect the people from the police but what are we spending to protect the people from themselves?

Now if You Ever

Think anyone or thing is in your way in life, use your imagination in a positive way to remove it or them out of your way. It is one of the most powerful tools God gives us all to do his will, if our hearts are in his will! Amen and Hallelujah

What it Means to Have Spiritual Skills

It is like the Lord gives you a pair of his boxing gloves that he has a present in and with that allows you to see the victories as he used you to take out of your way the opponent, Satan. He tries to set you up to win a fight of a spiritual kind. That can't happen if you are not in the fight representing the Lord. There is a new way of thinking that will be explained in an upcoming book titled *All Peoples Handbook*.

New Book News

Spiritual skills show you how to protect others (as what is done with my writing) with the power of and love in the Lord. It is somewhat at times, the opposite of what the new added dose that teaches ways to let God's protection fall on you with his intervention.

From a Gift I know That Belongs to You I Can Pass Along

I feel the Lord gives everyone a gift. I sometimes feel like mine is to make things look like a jewel in the desert that brings more meaning to peoples' lives to keep spreading the love.

In order to not get left out of this body of justice that works for all, there is such an unfortunate thing that happened when so many soldiers got caught up in the "ism" of mental health and lost a part of their spiritual well-being. The somewhat dependence of mankind in the process of a treatment created by Uncle Sam that at one time added to the blinding that may or may not have helped is out of order in a way that the blind people cannot lead the people to a promise land that they can find for themselves with the light to lead them out of their problems. That is why this help was created for service men and women. That is why the book was put together titled *The Unwounding of U.S. Service Men and Women*.

Public Notice

To understand people so they can understand themselves is all I can do going forward.

Getting out of the void-noid pipeline is something we must learn to do. First, by knowing it is there, next letting the Lord show you a way out. This will give you the strength you need to get it right. You will find more about this in upcoming books.

Zone Out to Zone In

One of the number one things people need to divide up is time out with themselves. It is a tool that lots of people do not use enough. For some that don't, it causes them to have issues because they don't think out the right action. Then they pay a price that causes too much on one level or another. This is what could be a partner to Satan and we don't need any of his tricks to trip us up along our pathway in life.

I Would Like to Think I Can Depend on You but Can You Depend on Yourself?

The facts are in and I am now in what could be said is a fight but if we see a good fight, shouldn't we get in it? To make it clearer, this one may be a spiritual fight that can only be won by the Lord. So our job is to do the right thing and cheer him on to victory, to receive a better education on how to look away from darkness to see the light because it will always be there. Go to the website, www.boundtoheaven.org to support this righteousness.

This may help you conquer the craziness of self before you learn how to not deal with the craziness of others.

There are people out in the world who think when they give money to the church they are paying them to do the job that they don't want to do or are not willing to do for themselves. So they pay to get away from not having to do it, but in heaven it is and will remain an empty account.

Last But Not Least

There are some people who think they have bought their way out of hell and paid their way into heaven with money on earth. Now can you become any less wise than that? If so, I really don't want to know.

Author's Note

I am a doer who believes that show beats tell all day long!

I have been working over half of my life learning to write, as an uneducated writer because I had the passion and calling.

The one issue I have is am I wrong about my thinking, because I am not perfect. But I do feel in my heart I can help change the course of history in a good way.

When I think of my writing it makes me think I shake some of the old food out to put in some soul food in people!

Muse-News

M-N

We can save a part of our young people's future with the work we are doing today.

M-N

Now, I say how many are left in the Lord's Superbowl? If you are one, I support you!

M-N

Do not produce a parado (Spanish word meaning motionless) in the way you think or talk within yourself.

M-N

To readers: out of the billions of books, what makes these special. Only we can answer that together.

M-N

Don't be blind to this sign. It is time to have happy people in a happy country.

Author's Note

Sometimes I feel I got left out of so much I don't know where I belong then you came along! Thank you so much. To learn more about what I am talking about go to website and get the books that help

I am not just one way with my vote, whether it is democratic or republican, the best person to do the job that is who I will vote for.

I Would Like to Say You Have My Vote

The road to the graveyard can be lonesome and long to those who pass judgment on others. Don't do it to yourself or anyone else.

Thank you for taking the time to read this information Bro. Tracy E. Bush

We can create a miracle of greatness at the end of the day once we are in order spiritually.

We Can Be Like David Against Goliath

It is a messed up system of b.s. we can conquer to make sense of it all.

When We All look to create a glimmer of hope for our country
we create a mountain of blessing to be shared.

This is a process that we need to be aware of on all levels of politics from councilmen and women, mayors, etc.

Now is the right time to create the death of "isms," such as political "isms" that are tied into towerism.

How many people could be perpetrating their love for America just to get something from it?

Do you have the offshore account of American money who doesn't invest back in the USA?

Now is the Best

Now is the time to turn this problem upside down and right side up and use that ounce of prevention the Lord has given as a blessing.

M-N

Developing a plan to convince people to stop accepting phony identification that belongs to others is necessary. Let's make our country free from this and the number one in the world in doing that. We don't deal with this kind of criminal activity more so than anyone else in other lands, showing this kind of love can conquer.

M-N
Know No

There are some things out there on the internet that I won't participate in that equated within a sense of a combination of evil. It is time to know the taboo level of thinking to not go along with.

M-N

What party do you think has the most towerism people in it? Republican, Democrat. We the people are the fact checkers that get the right news out for all to know.

The presence that is in this manual which has and can be like the miracle of healing of a part of the nation that need the help as if the balm of Gilead has been placed upon my heart that is supposed to be shared with the world in through book.

M-N

Prophesying the new level of love is permitted.

If and when you go to or talk about the harvest, which harvest are you going to or talking about?

Author's Note

I once knew a friend named Donald and his father named was John called him Duck. He did that because when we were out at a body of water he could play or swim in, he would always Duck his head under the water. It reminds me of another Donald that needed to act like a duck and get out of the ay and let the politicians do their job.

People

Now look around and see the past and the present and the towers who stack up upon one another that have done, things that are not right. We as voters can stop them from becoming elected officials in our land.

Take Notice

The most well-known tower that ever lived at one time in history was the popes. They were so crazy they said you could not go to the Lord unless you went through them. They had so much of themselves out of control, there were two popes at the same time, as if they were twin towers at odds with who will rule the house of God they presided over until it was settled.

Now if at a time a pope could be a dope, we may not know who will be the one who falls into that category of people. Now let us remember we all can change from an unheavenly state of mind, thanks to God's grace and mercy.

Therefore if it can affect the popes because there were two at one time in history there is still hope for us all. Now what do you wear on your persona that only the Lord sees, a set of bull horns or a halo. Now is the time for politicians to stop fighting mankind's facts that state I am politically correct when it is not morally correct.

Out of All

Out of all who have the real abilities to lead the country to keep it healthy, wealthy and wise that has an unselfish love that won't get influenced by the special interest groups the lobbyist, etc., only God knows but we must do our best to see the truth in the candidates because the world depends on us not just the land we live in. Thank you, my people Bro. Bush using the biggest four letter word on the planet, love.

I Don't Have Every Answer

The dilemma I have also is does Donald really want to be president or does he want the people to be aware of what they are getting for a president for their vote? Now do we see our best bet on the hill let's be for real? Now may we understand that we can cross out the sins of the fathers in government to not clog up the future with the past.

This is a real manifestation of a part of the legacy of mankind that is all dressed up and ready for you take it with you. I have no need to go along it has an identity of its own I see through a vision I was given through my faith in the pursuit of the love in life I know that came from my father in heaven. Therefore, count me in or cut out of your mind sight but never forget about the father's wishes; from a sometimes lonesome soldier for the Lord.

There is no better time to take some of Satan's secrets out of the darkness that has harmed mankind for centuries or decades or even millennia, to reveal a new lighthouse full of love that is needed by mankind before the Lord comes back to claim his church, which is his bride.

New Days

Now is the time to claim and share the richness of the world without the wealth of money to come between it.

See and Know

Voting power of the people of our country has taken on a new face that it has never before. Therefore, it may be somewhat of a spiritual war that we can win with the Lord.

This has been a cumbersome journey to keep on track to do the will of the Lord to try to help change the establishment. But, it will come to pass, I say Lord thank you for waking me and giving me the right state of mind. At times, I felt as if I was running ahead of a hurricane to warn the people to prevent them from a disaster.

Let the words of this writing become a part of our meditation of the heart and be acceptable in the sight of God.

Let this become an offering that had no sin in it, rather given out of friendship with God.

As we celebrate God's gifts in our lives, let us remember what Jesus said in Matthew 25:40 and the King will answer and say to them, 'Assuredly, I say to you, inasmuch as you did it to one of the least of these My brethren, you did it to Me.' In verse 45, He said, 'then He will answer them saying, Assuredly, I say to you, inasmuch as you did not do it to one of the least of these, you did not do it to Me.'

This is A Crisis; It Is an Emergency

To continue to not do the will of God will only bring misfortune to our country. The Lord is fed up. That is why the leaders and people are being warned.

To know the complete understanding of this problem that you may not find in this book, you can go to the book, _The Recovery of the U.S. Government_. To end such towerism by leaders of other countries we must show a change. As an example, there was a shah and his wife who had towerism. There was a president who supported a family that was blinded or just did not care because they had the problem, the list is endless. There are those in the past who have caused the people they led to lose out on many blessings even as the dictator in Africa who had towerism. Now who in leadership in our land has this?

I would also like to mention the individuals in the world soccer committee who are portraying towerism and the drug cartels that are haunted with it. We can dishonor those who are dis-servicing the sport. We can stop towering intellectuals who defraud the people. There are levels that are high in power financially and those who are not so high. The biggest set of people in the world who are terrorists are the people affiliated with and in charge of the world soccer league. Know this to be true; say no to that. That is enough so stop the corruption in all lands that reflects back on America.

The drug sellers are hit with it. The jewel thieves, the internet thieves are a few examples. There are people all over the world who have it and what happens is the less fortunate get hurt by it.

What can we do about this worldly sickness? Again, I say start first in the USA to stop being a part of it and maybe it will show others the way out of it.

How to Begin Taking Out or Down Towerism

We can begin to take down towerism with prayer for freedom of this bondage, biblical study that grants freedom. This wisdom is for the people who want a change in America and know we need it also. It will help the president do a better job for sure. When we do this, it will have a trickle up effect to help stop the problem of towerism.

Do not let this information make things jumbled up for you; let it make you humble.

It is an offensive smell that may be a new kind of calamity for reality to understand the principals involved in this message that are good for the people.

I say this to make it clear that politicians and business people alike have to stop dealing with anyone in foreign lands who has towerism; the people who control people have it, the people who are in charge of people who work others in sweatshops and those who have businesses in other lands that let them be dictated to by individuals with towerism. We must break the ties with any nation or country in the entire world who displays this in order for us to be a prosperous people in the eyes of God and not just want to prosper between another. This must stop.

People stuck in an invisible state of biblical bias that need to learn of a way out

Don't Turn a Deaf Ear or Blind Eye to This Truth

The Lord is fed up with this in His people. Anyone that is involved with it will be held accountable.

This book will help prevent some of the problems in Congress. It can help stop all the disagreements within and between both parties: to break stalemates; to stop filibusters; to aid in crossing the divide to act like a bridge over troubled water.

There is one big issue that most people have with the government who are under the guidelines of the law that was created by people who have towerism. It reflects so much upon them that created these laws, that is the taxation that the less fortunate are required to pay and the rich and wealthy have less to pay. This is such an unfortunate thing that the government allows this to continue and it needs to change. The ideology is somewhat backward in their thinking but that is what a system that is put together by individuals with towerism does.

It started long ago when rulers such as pharaohs, kings even popes had towerism. The problem can also be found with CEO's of drug companies who sell products at inflated rates to consumers, as well as banks and other loan agencies who lend money at outrageous interest rates. This seems to be done because of personal greed.

This is an old problem that has phased out in existence that mankind acts like it doesn't want to change straight up!

Being Spiritually in Line is Better
Than Being Intellectually Inclined!

This level of presence by identifying a problem and naming it can change the attitude of the people in the country for the better and knowing we can join in to lift the people in a more joyful way to not only take the veil off of darkness but do something about it. For those who sit in high place it also brings them back down to earth in order for them to build a light house and take down their towers to replace it with light that is shot out to the land we are not under the Roman rule with a trap that is set by them that creates a sea of red.

Author's Note

All the writing I do is about spiritual growth as a human being that is something we all need to do.

M-N

This one possible thought can move the whole to a new level of dignity of presence in the world.

Pinpoint it Then Stop it

Goal: to take towerism out of our government and the people who use it in our land.

What Power Can Do

We all can do better knocking down the unseen walls that Satan has put in front of us on all levels.

In the book it is the people who take on the government to improve it. We can defeat the lobbyist and special interest groups that represent the people with towerism in the name of the Lord.

What is one of people's biggest problems? They don't want to use good advice sometimes and don't want to face up to the truth and what to do about it; learn to not be like this kind of problem to yourself.

The stopping of towerism is and can be one of the greatest parts of healing the nation that we all can share in as a village.

Together We Rise

We are stopping and stamping out the demonic spirits of towerism that take away from the progress of people in all nations.

Defeating Wrong
Author's Note

One way to defeat wrong by learning to fear not the wrong thing as was done in my life when it came down to my gift of writing. I was laughed at, talked about and said I wouldn't be able to rub two nickels together for a living from writing and it somewhat affected me. It wasn't the silver and gold I was after but to fulfill my life and its purpose that was all, even if I never made a dime!

Towerism has a little brother called egoism. Need I say more, other than that both are trouble-makers.

Could this be a part of a polluted dream or nightmare?

A Real Truth to Trust

From this day forward let's do it for our country again. We do it for our country without bias to protect us from the thought of an act of any kind of terrorist. We can use the spiritual intervention that gives foresight that can warn us. I was used by the love I had for my mother when she was alive. How did this work? It was revealed to me in a dream. I acted on it before another murder was committed.

I know of pathways I write about that may help others dream a blessing of safety for themselves and others.

This will help stop lots of politricks that is going on in the houses of government to help for the goodness of all people.

If direction is what we need, then it is direction that we have.

The Beginning

If this writing has helped you look up to the sky and thank the Lord, Thank God!

Is this one of the latest and true statements we can listen to that brings honesty?

Do we have to stay stuck in the middle of the messages that certain people are putting out in the media? A no contested element of talking back and forth has occurred between two parties. One party that may be building towers, the other party that is surrounded by a wall. Which one is right or wrong? Only you know the answer but I say the right kind of fence may do but who am I? I am not in charge of anything to do with that. The only thing I am in charge of is my opinion and my vote. I'll look at this as a quiet storm that was not designed to hurt anyone.
Therefore it reflects on a poem I wrote. Whether the weather be hot, whether the weather be cold.
Weather the weather, whatever the weather, whether you like it or not.

The problem in life is so many people want others to get caught up in their peopleism, that needs to stop.

I used a historical and biblical landscape of information to produce the facts in a layman terminology that can be used to bridge an understanding of wisdom that mankind can see the future in a better way than what it is looking at now that creates change with the least resistance.

There was a president who passed a bill giving 28 million to the urban league but he was a tower that fell down.

Dr. God

Doctor God can become a spiritual surgeon to repair the spiritual illness in anyone who comes to him in need. Towerism doesn't mean you have a bad heart but the principals you use are out of line with people who have a need you may be able to fulfill. Make it known it was never intended for the rich to keep getting richer in no land and the poor to get poorer. We can't fix it all but we can do better.

A sign of towerism: a person who has human principals which leaves God out.

It Ain't Me

We the people write/right the legislation that is governed by the Lord to let all His people know that they will not perish in the famine that was created by mankind because of the fall of the towers that outplayed its hand. We look to make this the first and only state in America that this misguidedness can happen in our union, to show what the sin-drome of the forefathers has caused. Up with us for the last time in the world's history, with the Lord's help I submit this to the people.

Help is on the way for the innocent. The fervent prayers of God's people will prevail. We honor this pledge on behalf of the Lord who sent us to represent him.

No man has the need to have fear of this. If they do, don't blame the Lord's messenger.

I would like to think that the words I write, which are inspired by God, will affect positive change to all people who read them.

We have the "we cans" now, the first, "we can" is to stop and confront the personal demons that have been producing outlandish behavior in our presence of being that we can no longer be a part of. Now we can stop the presence outlandish behavior in our beings as a people who are developing a higher level of agape love.

Now are you voting as the Lord would want you to vote or are you doing it just to make yourself or someone else feel good just to be able to say "I did it for them" or others.

One of the biggest problems with the people who are infested with towerism is one who leaves a job before they have cleaned up their mess.

This wording is to help the grown get and become stronger and to keep itself from itself and the people, to stop the unseen enemy can become a part of the element of being human. Facing the truth doesn't come easy at times because if it doesn't show up like an outward reflection of a person who thinks they are clean and are not but have a sickness and live with it like nothing is wrong. They are so wrong because of a so-called good life they have that came by way of the price they had to pay to the prince of darkness.

Therefore, if you get an itch to take a notion to your life, know that it isn't worth it to live as a person with towerism, it can cause a kind of inertia of bliss, no pun intended.

Towerism is one of mankind's sicknesses inspired by Satan. The time has come for us to identify and fix it before it destroys a part of the world, that it has not already, more so the people in the world that the fallout lands upon who gets hurt by it.

Forgiveness is a key to fixing it but it can't happen unless it is stopped, because it has an affect like Sodom and Gomorrah, with a stench that displeases the Lord's nostrils, along with mankind also at this time in history.

People have to draw their own conclusions about this message. I can't convince you of anything.

If anyone wants to know how to get out of the "ism" attack that is upon you, pray and receive the right one, a God "ism."

For All the Tomorrows

It is time to stop some people from turning their back on themselves, including the reversal of the Judas in self if you have it. The notice of this comes at times

46

when some people lose everything and want to harm themselves or a loved one.

We Are Not But People

The people in the country are fed up but they shouldn't give up and let life trumple them.

The fact is bureaucratic thieves and all other thieves cause a loss of wealth that can be used to help prevent crime in all communities. People want to take the wrong way out with drug use, they hear the ongoing waste of tax money and the misuse of money, resources is a downer for the citizens.

They say beware of who may be sitting in high places, because we don't ever want to look like the government of Brazil, or other countries in the world, with corruption.

Beware of your giving and your taking. If you don't give it to the poor you don't give to the Lord; noting that we may be in the same place but a different universe.

Towerism will suck you in to suck you up to a place in your state of mind that will kick you around and you may never get down from it until you fall apart. It doesn't discriminate whether you are rich or poor but it hits the water in a way they may not see or know that leaves them somewhat blind to towerism's biggest enemy, humility. That is a sickness by itself that is so unfortunate, no matter how some may fake it because they have nothing in common with the common man in the sight of the Lord.

Know this: there are certain things that mankind can't get or get rid of except by way of the father. Satan will give you everything to keep you content in his spirit that can reside in people. No one that is exempt from this unless they possess the favor of the Lord that is on His side and in His will.

We can stop the ramped of this that has been running wild through the earth, like a fire at its roots, in order for it to burn out. Amen and hallelujah

The Lord is not disappointed in anyone who fills their cup up to cause it to overflow, but if they keep the overflow, it is a part of their self damnation. Therefore, undamn yourself, it will not benefit you and you would be better off rich in spirit and poor in the sight of a bank account that may add an eternity of pain that follows you forever.

Stopping the destruction of souls of mankind that gave out hell sentences, like in a not knowing state of action without informing the blind at the same time when their freedom was placed on doorsteps and walked on like a sickness of towerism or selfishness and greed. Now what does this have to do with my way of growing out of this dilemma? It is the consequences of no change, which is needed to grow out of this dilemma.

As I try to navigate the way out for others to see a silver lining in a cloud sent from heaven as a pathway of thinking that unearthed an injustice as was done by a white woman who wrote the book Uncle Tom's Cabin. This helped change the hearts of millions who saw the need to free people and to help understand the level of need to see their way out of a kind of darkness that we walked over without seeing the light. At the end of the process of growth we as people need to not only be made aware of for ourselves but to be shared with our fellow man.

Taking note that some of the people in cahoots that are white are still unseen and in a way enslaved by Satan, and are chained up by him on a spiritual level of not being able to grow beyond their insecurities about black people. They need our help as if it is or has been in the past as if it was needed with the writing of the message in the book UTC, even though we know there are some who don't like black people; but I don't mind because I am minding my father's business that is in heaven.

Therefore, I implore you to feel the same way because all of our job is to do the will of the father and fill up heaven with all of mankind that is in accordance to the will of him, because his color of us will be one that is seen in the light that has claimed his right while on earth before the temple of their body is committed to the grave.

For this cause it compelled me to come together as a people with the incentive of being color blind as was imbedded in me as a child by my grandfather, telling me I was a white boy at my earliest of youth and as he stood a six-feet plus, light-skinned man. So I think am I a part of the missing link of the past, present and future that got found before my time to leave earth? I think so thanks to my Lord and Savior Jesus Christ.

There is one personal issue that troubled me, did I have to drive a part of my life out of me by way of the youth I had to grow into the maturity to develop the way out for others to go? I don't know, but if so it is okay because the young heart replaced it all at this time and more so I believe after death. Therefore, I said hallelujah is forever and I will bless the Lord. Note: I thank the many shoulders I had to stand upon to see the light and not just the darkness.

A Call to Duty

Now if money of all kinds becomes useless on the earth, what can we do to increase the body of Christ? Even though it is not a part of our history, act like this anyway. Then see where the Lord places you. You might be surprised where you end up and/or belong go now with the joy of the Lord in your heart.

The reason I use this scenario is not to show up prejudice but to give a non-evasive objective that will get attention to the seriousness of what I am telling you. The fact is the people of wealth are in the majority are Caucasian people, in the way I have depicted the information. Even though there is no color barrier in towerism.

My Confession

It didn't come to me at first, but when it did, I almost fell out of my seat. I learned I first wrote for myself to learn what I didn't know. Then it came to me to share it. Maybe someone else may find some new truth to take along with them in life to gain a new kind of truth to live with, within and out of them.

What we are doing is getting people in a presence of not exactly like the somewhat freedom of prejudice but the freedom from the demons of towerism, with an opening up of themselves to let it out to go from the ungodliness in the spirit of mankind.

Advice

We must all learn how to tell each other to listen to what we tell each other next. Everyone has a little of this towerism in them, but not everyone lets it take them out in a space that can harm others.

Warning

Beware because some people in high places do come as thieves in the night but it is blinding in the daylight also.

No man can subdue or create a substandard to any man's life that has been blessed to perform a duty for the Lord. He or she that carries out the will of the Lord is equal to any man, no matter who it is or what they are doing. It is just another branch of the tree of life in the body of Christ. Now, if you think you are exalted higher than anyone who is equal to you in the Lord's eyes, then you need to get down off of your plateau even if it is made out of gold. As it was said, if you exalt yourself you will be made low.

What has been presented by this writing? It is a way to have a good structure to work through a program with possible solutions, to supply to understand read it again until you get it.

Learn to learn the follower in you and do not be afraid of being in tune with who is on first and make sure you think of the big picture. There is a home base and you can get there without the presence of hell and high water that can burn or drown you.

Pray to come out of that tower and become humble. Then watch to see how much better you are and feel.

When you are fixing towerism, you are helping to fix every level of America's problems that have something wrong with it, believe it or not, but still you can take it for what it is worth. It is for your own good.

M-N

If you can identify it you can eliminate it; if you cannot, it is usually trouble.

M-N

How would you like to be a part of taking down a multitude of towers at one time? Think about it, you may get the opportunity one day, before you know it.

How would you like to be a part of stopping a terrorist plot to harm your fellow countrymen and women? Just imagine how many children's smiles can be kept safe along with their laughter, dream about it.

I am not afraid to know "no." I do believe in me about that.

It is time to fork over all the aristocratic b.s. out of your life you want to share with others. Once we get this done it may be a bigger step for mankind than standing on the moon.

If you do not know how towerism was created you can find the meaning in the book *The Recovery of the U.S. Government*.

By the time you complete this book you will have grown above towerism with your heart in a way that will let you soar above the clouds far away from hell holds. Also knowing wellness, mentally and spiritually, to a new kind of peace within.

All editing of this book was done in house by BTHPM to assure the development of strategies of the book's complete presentation that doesn't seem normal. It may only be because the book may not totally seem to be nonfiction. A part of the message has come to this world from another place in time. I thank you for understanding.

Now if you take one letter that is a "t" and replace it with a "c" it might be a key way to help the large part of the nation with healing so we can start to come together like even better than before.

This book may somewhat put people to work in a way that they have to put the picture together, with it showing a pathway to follow in order to see the beauty that it has within to help bring anyone to a new happiness with a new kind of son sunshine to see. To know sinning takes things apart like science does. Spirituality puts things together, so we can make a pilgrimage to put things together and not tear things apart; this I pray!

Now to bring about the blessed understanding I can when it comes down to a spiritual warfare, that may be going on in someone's life. It is not to be depicted as it is seen or illustrated in the movies.

It is somewhat on a level where when most people may be going in and out of one it is like a silent killer. It doesn't want people to identify with it at all. It will disguise itself and make people think they are in charge of themselves and their actions all by themselves. That is totally wrong; some people are taken advantage of before they know it and leaves them wondering how come they did something like harm someone and the first thing they will say is I didn't plan to do that, but Satan did plan it for you to do it if he had a chance to cause you to take action because you put yourself in a position he knows you were unprotected to be in by the opening up of your emotions that had no protection with the Lord's covering.

Now the other level of destruction may come in agreement with Satan in warfare with Satan to cause harm by way of a power struggle between parties. Now may your mind, heart and spirit beware of the presence of Satan that can try to harm you and sneak up on you like the invisible presence of the carbon monoxide fumes.

The big production that happens in the heavens during the first warring disagreement is now out of sight and in a sense out of mind that picks a perfect time to strike like lightning out of the sky whether it is light, dark, dry or raining.

Know now that we are protected in a capacity of love in every state of mind we go through. Therefore, enjoy your coming and going in life in the truth of trusting the love you carry for all people in your heart. Then you bless the Lord.

The greatest defense that the Lord gives anyone who is in a presence of what could be a physical war to be able to sense his presence to stop and walk away before it escalates before Satan joins two people into one way because it is sometimes just one person Satan has a hold of and people have a better chance to not get tied into one fight. But if there is a weapon all Satan wants is for one to harm the other

My thanks goes out to all my family in and of humanity, bad guys too because you can change once you or someone else figures out how to show the way how to become free.

Take Note

If any one of these examples seem familiar, it is only a reflection of what could be upward of an uncountable number of people throughout history that we have known of that made us laugh and smile and even cry with them in ways that they had a somewhat undetectable control or attraction that was in some kind of way irresistible to them. At the same time, they were unknowing that they had a dark side that was unhealthy at some point to other people in ways that were undetectable.

Now the crazy part is, at one time history it was not okay to display towerism but as an example we can look at slavery and what it represented; towerists who were to keep for itself underground. Believe it or not it was as much as he or it could in another standard of darkness that he persuaded mankind to adapt to on the down-low.

Therefore, in saying all of this, what can or must be done to stop its future? If you think or know someone who may have towerism, no matter who they are or what they have, ask the Lord to demagnetize you from them. It will help you see straight and get away from under their spell and help them free themselves from whatever hook that Satan has on them in life that might cost them their life when their earthly life is over.

Today and always know that you don't have to accept the skull and cross bone packages with love if it is a part of towerism in life because some things usually don't end right in one way or another.

Perception

It calls for a trumpectomy for those trumpees who have trumpitis. Now what does the duck have? Towerism.

Now can both parties accept that right amount of wrong has gone on long enough to bring out the truth in congress and both parties change some of their ways?

My concern is I am not a Republican at this time but I would at least like to see a fair fight without Satan weighing in with his people that could harm everyone. Now this is how we all can bless the Lord. Let's keep it out of the wrong and we can try to make it right.

It will be better to take a bruising and
keep on cruising than to not take a trumpectomy!

If you are a republican and don't want to allow the front-runner of the party to be a duck you are guaranteeing to not let him win with this methodology. With him as a leader, that is what it will be like for the country, we will be sitting ducks right alongside him!

There are a few paragraphs within the last chapters that were needed in this book to fulfill the understanding of an upcoming book titled *All Peoples Handbook*, that gives the wisdom to become blessed with the ability to receive spiritual skills and what they can be used to achieve to become a blessing to others.

M-N

If the truth makes you weak in the knees then use that to get down on your knees to pray and not let it work its way up to a heart attack.

M-N

Someone has to champion the cause. Why not you and me?

M-N

Can I be in some kind of personal anomaly? A place in space that you become locked into.

A way to level the playing field: by not allowing the "want to be" a member of the establishment" make a name for themselves or their ego.

Face the nation: with the guidance to give them not only want you think they want to hear just to pacify them but keep it real and tell it like it is.

M-N

One of the main things to consider is the respect ability of a president if some don't have it they should not lead. Push to get the duck out of the race.

M-N

Now to prevent the past from repeating itself we are in need of a lot more wisdom than we have been living by in our lives.

M-N
This Can Work

If we start from the top and work our way down to fix a number of problems in the USA because we are balkanized the presence of the phases of work to be done with one's self first.

A Note to the Wise

Now in these days do we really have to take sides all of the time? Why can't we learn to go with the flow to what we know as the right thing to do? Think about it. To prevent the people in the republican party to have a warfare and it hasn't yet become a full fledge war.

Having Dollars

To lessen the cost of your champion work it at a level of taking more of the voters by revealing a truth about you upon that makes one change sides the cost factors are less and you win more votes on the side.

Therefore who can or are you thinking you should trust first? Then make a single phase of work to help the republicans who have the biggest problems with towerism.

Make a single phase of work just for republican to stop the clump raise funds with it.

We are not picking the lesser of two evils but the best person for the job.

Now with this knowledge people can stop being afraid of changing the political agenda ending the part that Satan has played, with putting his one-half cent in: that has now been revealed!

The Dangers in America We Can Fix, II

Don't be blind to this sign. Get your download of eBooks on Amazon.com. Search Bro. Tracy Bush, search and visit www.boundtoheaven.org. It is time to have happy people in a happier country.

Just because someone makes more money than you, doesn't mean they are smarter than you!

Show Me The Way

Once we remove Satan's principals, mankind can have a fair fight among themselves.

It does not take a genius figure out this development of common sense.

A Lighthouse as A Reflection of the White House

Annex

Start again
A future to be had

There is blood in the pen of the writing I do to stop the bloodshed of the people. Every day is a chance to make things right in our life until the beginning of the rest of it.

Goal list

I will not let the love inside of me die. Love is power that teaches us to grow beyond the circumstances of life's trials and tribulations that come with the training we live with daily.

How do we stop man's unnatural hands that he develops to do harm to himself and others? With love the keys to wisdom start with love.

Don't be a part of Supremacy crimes are hyper masculine people who are out of control because You are inescapable you can't get away from you even in death

Because we need Conservatism of our self to create adjudicate in our life.

Therefore it will cost a little but you may get more than some are willing to deal with

This is the therapy we need to exorcise false hope

If you believe in something or someone and you cross the bridge called false hope and it is not all that its built up to be, then the cracks start to set in to end the hope.

Now I will put you on a road that will get you back across but it will take your faith to change the problem with IN people once they get across they don't want to make themselves seem as if they are a fool of some kind. They also feel a sense of being lost in a place that is uncomfortable I call the V-N sin-drome.

Therefore if they want to go back across the bridge they may feel like it will cave in or fall down. What do some people do about that feeling? This answer will give you an idea of two groups of people if you are the kind of person who can't stand being wrong you may raise some kind of hell. Or if you are the other kind of person you will want to become a martyr of some kind to a degree that you raise up so much hell it opens a door to let you in as terrorists do.

This is the fast false hope that isn't real. It is a figment of the imagination that is a part of the void-noid. Therefore, the thought of falling into the void-noid is an ungodly powerful way to stay lost. That is why this bridge of understanding that makes up a part of the love factor can stop or kill fear to make people able to cross back over aging and get back on track. People soon forget we owe our eternal allegiance to no man and if he doesn't know himself he isn't worth following.

The belief we have to know ourselves has to be questioned sometime daily and if we can't find the right answer we can only rely on a higher power to give it or use to use. There is nothing wrong with questioning yourself in times of having a troubled mind. It is the truth of wisdom that will only create the sanctuary of peace to make your cup overflow.

Honesty is the best policy but whose honesty do you have in your life yours, mine, someone else's, or the Lord's?

To and For All People

Once you get your heart right you will not have to fear going back over the bridge and foremost laying down the weapons of war.

A New Beginning and not a deadly end!

Now, who wants to obtain achievement when they can obtain fulfillment in their life?

My opinion may be wrong and I can't rely on any one side totally as a winner. That is why I say let's look at the whole picture. I am only trying to keep people safe long enough for them to be able to see their eternity!

Satan has a way of activating people. This is the way to deactivate them. People have to stop the problem of wanting to act like asses who want to take others on the wrong kind of ride.

The seeds are being planted and
all you have to do is let it work for you.

The thing called trumpitis causes people to let a hole be put in their soul. That can stop so the good cannot keep slipping out of them.

Do not get sad or made when it seems like you have been made out of a chump by a man named trump that leaves people in a dump. Now before we look at the future because of the new people in charge, we must remember that lots of people will be disappointed about the loss.

That is why this book has become a bridge across a dam that wants to break to flood the atmosphere with hatred that leaves to a pathway of people who the first chance they get to protest at rallies to make things worse for the country.

This pound of prevention can create a cure that leads to a miracle of change to bless the land of America.

I believe there is a 70% chance that the republican candidate will lose. Therefore to ease the pain of millions of people this can be a pill to swallow in order to keep the country moving in the right direction.

What can or does this say? We should look forward to working together with the democratic and republican parties to forge a better and newer America because it is not about the two parties. It is about the people and the needs that are to be fulfilled.

Bottom line: I can only say for myself I feel the voters in the republican party will possibly be more upset because of the way the party leaders feel will cause a kind of uprising of negativity that all people can head off because it is Satan's influence that wants to create an ungodly justice just to put pain in peoples' lives. We should pray for all candidates regardless, because anyone can change!

Common Sense

It is better to have a tally on the mistakes someone has made than the mistakes someone is going to make. The bottom line is, we should forgive people and stop the prejudices.

The negative perspective

People can Reform the Attitude They Have Against Self

Towerism for some can be like a drug. They get hooked on it and it has the power to pull people in that could be called a state of trumpecstasy, that is a state of unseen but real kind of high that creates an invisible effect of A undetected presence of an endorphin movement in people who are powerless against it.

Keeping it real I know the country is tired and fed up with the same old hill top bull and we deserve a change. People were somewhat surprised and wouldn't you know who comes along and beats out everyone at the table and made others look like jack legs, with a top hat that can put on a show to fool the people who think they can never be fooled. That is right, the representative of a towerist faction.

Therefore at the same time spreading a blinding kind of existence that can make some think you may need to get an exorcism before you can get yourself out of the spell. Hell, I wanted to jump on the band wagon but I can't. I know the truth.

People also may think he is going to be some kind of miracle in the world for them and he may wind up with his inexperience putting the country in the belly of the whale or a battle of some kind. The USA doesn't want or need who want to know the truth.

Ohio, and the entire country don't need to have trumpitis and for those who already have it, they can get a spiritual trumpectomy.

I hold nothing personally against the Trump. He is the best example I have to help people see and know the point that is being made.

This may have been said more than once

Understanding what towerism is that functions in America without limitations that should not be. Also there is some information in the book to help you feel better about the loss of the election if the republican lose to help end the trumpitis with a therapy called a trumpectomy with a plan that gives spiritual wellness to all people, as well as learning that accepting towerism gives a better way of understanding how to end terrorism because lots of "isms" are dangerous.

You Can't Con Anyone Who Isn't Con-able

There have been blessings received from the work Tracy has done before! During the RNC in 2016, he promoted peace with _A Peace Offering for the Police and the _People, as well as others books to help stop confusion.

I think the leaders that are trapped on the wrong side of the bridge and can't get back by themselves can use our help. If you know one or more share this with them, they are also human and no one is perfect.

Philippians 4:17
17. Not that I seek the gift, but I seek the fruit that abounds your account.

Acts 20:24
24. But none of these things move me; nor do I count my life dear to myself, so that I may finish this race with joy, and the ministry which I received from the Lord Jesus, to testify to the gospel of the grace of God.

Thank you to everyone!